The subject matter and vocabulary have been selected with expert assistance, and the brief and simple text is printed in large, clear type.

Children's questions are anticipated and facts presented in a logical sequence. Where possible, the books show what happened in the past and what is relevant today.

Special artwork has been commissioned to set a standard rarely seen in books for this reading age and at this price.

Full-colour illustrations on all 48 pages give maximum impact and provide the extra enrichment that is the aim of all Ladybird Leaders.

Where the male and female birds are almost alike, the words 'cock' or 'hen' are not shown against an illustration.

Pages 36 and 37 show a selection of birds, male and female.

See back of book for index.

A Ladybird Leader
song birds

written and illustrated by John Leigh-Pemberton

Publishers: Ladybird Books Ltd . Loughborough
© Ladybird Books Ltd 1974
Printed in England

The lapwing's call is 'pee-wit'.
Peewit is another name for this bird.

Bird calls

Most birds make two kinds of sound.
One of these is the bird's call.
This is usually a short note.
It shows alarm. It gives warning.
It calls the young.

What does the song mean ?

Each kind of bird has its own song.
When this blackbird sings, he says,
'I am a blackbird.
This is my territory.
I am looking for a mate'.

Singing in flight

Birds usually sing when perching.
Many birds also sing when flying.
The skylark sings as it flies upwards
and as it hovers.

Skylark

The skylark's song
is a very loud, warbling sound.
Its song lasts a long time.

How do they do it?

The calls and songs of birds
come from their throats.
Even whistling sounds
are made in this way.

The nuthatch gives
a long, clear whistle.

The wren's song

The cock wren
has a very loud song.
It is a clear,
rippling sound.
This tiny bird sings
from a low perch or when flying.
The female wren also sings.
She has a very quiet song.

The dunnock or hedge sparrow

Most birds sing only in spring
and summer.

But the wren and the dunnock
sing all the year.

The dunnock's song is short,
quiet and very sweet.

The hen robin's song

Usually only cock birds sing.
But the hen robin also sings.
During the autumn
she has her own territory.
She warns off other birds with her son

Cock

The redstart
a summer visitor to Britain.

The redstart's song
is rather like the robin's.

It is a short, musical warble.

The song ends suddenly
with an odd, jingling noise.

The nightingale
a summer visitor to Britain

The nightingale sings at night
and in the daytime.
The beautiful song is loud and clear.
A loud 'jug-jug-jug' sound
is followed by many rapid notes
and a long 'peeyew' sound.

The song thrush

'Did he do it?
He did, he did, he did'.
This is what the song
of the song thrush sounds like.
He usually sings it again and again.

The mistle thrush
is larger than the song thrush

This bird's loud song is often sung
from the top of a tree.

The song is in three parts.

These are repeated many times.

The blackbird

Hen

Cock

The blackbird sings a real tune.
During the summer he adds to his song.
He experiments with it
and improves it.

The starling
a bird with
many voices

The starling's song is a mixture.

It is made up of warbles, whistles, chirping and clicking noises.

Starlings can also copy the songs and calls of other birds.

A chirping song

Not all bird songs are beautiful.

The house sparrow's song is made up of many harsh notes.

Sounds like 'chilp', 'chissick' and 'cheap', together form a sort of song.

Sparrows live in flocks.

They often sing together in a noisy chorus.

Hen

Cock

Crested tit

Coal tit

Long-tailed tit

The tit family

Tits live in small flocks.
Blue tits stay together,
long-tailed tits
stay together, and so on.
They often use their calls
to keep a flock together.

Marsh tit

Willow tit

Blue tit

'Tissy-tissy', 'zit-zit' or 'pitchu'
are the sort of sounds they make.

The song of some tits
is just a little trill.

The song of others
is made of their call notes.

The willow tit does not sing often,
but it is the best singer.

The great tit

The largest of the tits is the great tit.
You will soon know its song.
It sounds like someone
sawing a piece of wood,
'Tee-chu, tee-chu, tee-chu'.

Pigeons and doves

Stock
dove

Turtle dove,
a summer visitor
to Britain

Pigeons and doves have songs
made up of cooing and purring sounds.
'Cooo-coo, coo coo, coo'
or 'roor-roor, roor-roor, roorrr'.

Rock
dove

Wood pigeon

25

Warblers

Warblers are pretty little birds.
They spend the winter
in Africa or in Asia.
In the spring they fly away
to cooler countries to breed.
Their beautiful songs are made up of
trills and warbling notes.

Cock

*The whitethroat,
one of the best-known
of the warblers*

The blackcap
another warbler

Hen

Cock

The blackcap sings
in April, May and June.

Of all the warblers,
the blackcap's song is one of the best.

After nesting, blackcaps return to Africa
in October.

The wood warbler

This bird has two songs.
One starts slowly and then gets faster
'Stip-stip stititititipp-swee'.
The other is 'whee-ou',
which is repeated many times.

Willow warbler and chiffchaff

Willow warbler

pale legs

Chiffchaff

dark legs

These two little birds look alike.

But their songs are quite different.

The chiffchaff sings,
'chiff-chaff, chiff-chaff, chiff-chaff',
over and over again.

The willow warbler's song starts softly.

It gets louder and lower,
then it fades away.

Reed warbler

Marsh warble.

Sedge
warbler

These little warblers are found
among reeds or in damp places.

Their songs are partly sweet notes
and partly harsh, rattling noises.

Some warblers copy the others' songs

A hidden singer

Some birds perch and sing
where they can be seen.

Others, like the garden warbler,
sing when hidden in a bush or tree.

The garden warbler has a quiet,
warbling song.

It is rather like the blackcap's song,
but lasts longer.

The Dartford warbler

Dartford warblers are rare.

A few live in parts of southern England

They stay there all the year.

The song is a bright, musical chatter,

often sung from the top of a gorse bus

Singing on the ground

Most birds sing when perched in a tree
or when flying.
The wheatear sings while standing
on a large stone or tuft of grass.

Cock

Hen

The stonechat and the whinchat

Cock

Stonechat
He often
sings in
flight

Cock

Whinchat

Blackbirds, redstarts,
nightingales, wheatears,
stonechats and
whinchats are all
members of the
thrush family

The stonechat's alarm call
is 'wee-chat, wee-chat-chat'.

Its song is a short, rapid warble
rather like that of the dunnock.

The whinchat's song
is much the same.

The flycatchers
summer visitors to Britain

Spotted
flycatcher

Pied
flycatcher

Cock

The spotted flycatcher
does not often sing.

Its song is weak and squeaky.

The pied flycatcher has a better song.
It sounds like: 'tree tree tree,
once more I come to thee.'

The dawn chorus

Birds wake up before it is light.
Every morning in spring and summer,
they start to sing at dawn.
This is called 'the dawn chorus'.

First one bird starts to sing.
One by one the others join in.
Each one sings in its territory
to warn off other birds.
When the sun is up they stop singing
and look for food.

The finch family

A finch is a seed-eating bird
with a strong beak.

Its song is mostly twittering notes.

Most finches sing when flying
and when perching.

Cock

In Britain, the chaffinch
is the best-known finch.

His call is 'pink-pink'.

Cock

Hen

The bullfinch

The bullfinch's song is rather weak.
But the call-note,
is a soft, piping 'dee-you'.
After the young have left the nest,
the hen also sings.

The greenfinch

Cock

The greenfinch's call
is a long drawn out 'tsweee' sound.

It sings for most of the year.

At nesting time, the cock sings
a special song.

The goldfinch

The call-note of the goldfinch
is a liquid, tinkling sound.
It sounds like 'tswitt-witt-witt'
or 'pickel-witt-it'.
The call is repeated to make a song.

The crossbill

Hen

Cock

Crossbills are finches
with special cross-over beaks
for getting seeds out of fir-cones.

Their call-note is a loud 'chup-chup',
often made when flying.

The call is part of the song.

The linnet

Cocks

Of all the finches,
the twittering song of the linnet
is one of the best.

Often, a flock of cock linnets
sing together in chorus.

The call-note is a soft 'tsooeet'.

The siskin and the redpoll

Cock

Siskin

Cock

Redpoll

Often these little finches
are seen together in small flocks.

Both have songs made up of
twitterings and trills.

These finches are found most often
in northern Britain and in Ireland.

The yellowhammer

'Little-bit-of-bread-and-no-cheese'.
That is what the squeaky song
of the yellowhammer
is said to sound like.

Cock

Some finches are called 'buntings'.
The yellowhammer is one of these.

The cuckoo's song

The well known 'cuckoo' sound
is made only by the male bird.

The song is sung while flying
or from a perch.

The female's song sounds like
bubbling water or a quiet chuckle.

The cuckoo's eggs

A female cuckoo lays
about twenty eggs each year.
She lays each egg in the nest
of another sort of bird.
The other bird thinks the egg is hers.
She hatches and feeds the young cuckoo.

The reed bunting

Cock

Buntings usually nest on the ground.
They sing from a low perch
but not often from a tree.

The reed bunting's song
is a shrill, tinkling sound,
'tweek-tweek-tweek-tititick'.

The corn bunting

The corn bunting sings his song
over and over again.

It begins with fast ticking noises.

The song ends with a sound
like the jingling of a bunch of keys.

Pipits and wagtails

Meadow pipit.

Cock

Cock

Pied wagtail

Grey wagtail

Cock

There are several kinds
of pipits and wagtails.

Of the birds that walk instead of
hopping, these are the smallest.

Their twittering songs
are usually sung while flying.

The smallest singer

Cock

The goldcrest is only 3½ inches
(8.9 cm) in length.

It is the smallest British bird.

The song is very shrill and feeble,
'cedar-cedar-cedar-sissu-pee'.

Bird	Length in cm	Where found	When seen	Page
Blackbird	25	Gardens, woods, towns	All the year	9, 19, 37
Bullfinch	14.5-16	Woods, gardens, orchards	All the year	39
Bunting, Corn	18	Hedges, farmland, downs	All the year	49
Reed	15	Reed beds, moors	All the year	48
Chaffinch	15	Gardens, hedges	All the year	8, 38
Chiffchaff	11	Woods, shrubberies, gardens	March to October	29
Crossbill	16.5	Fir forests	All the year	42
Cuckoo	33	Woods, moors, hills	March to September	46, 47
Dove, Rock	33	Coasts, fields, caves	All the year	25
Stock	33	Woods, fields, cliffs	All the year	25
Turtle	27	Gardens, hedges, valleys	April to October	25
Dunnock	14.5	Gardens, hedges	All the year	13, 37
Flycatcher, Pied	13	Woods, gardens, near water	April to September	35
Spotted	14	Woods, gardens, parks	April to October	35
Goldcrest	8.9	Woods, hedges, gardens	All the year	51
Goldfinch	12	Gardens, open country	All the year	41
Greenfinch	14.5	Gardens, farmland	All the year	40
Lapwing	30	Farmland, moors	All the year	4
Linnet	13.5	Gorse, bushes, gardens	All the year	43
Nightingale	16.5	Woods, bushes	April to September	16
Nuthatch	14	Woods, gardens, parks	All the year	11
Pigeon, Wood	41	Woods, fields, gardens	All the year	25
Pipit, Meadow	14.5	Moors, fields, seashore	All the year	50
Redpoll	13-15	Birch trees, near water	All the year	44
Redstart	14	Woods, rocks, hills	April to October	15
Robin	14	Gardens, woods	All the year	5, 7, 14, 26